Starting Off Strong

Primary

Starting Off Strong

Primary

Beginning
Shared Inquiry™
in Your Classroom

Junior Great Books®
Read-Aloud

The Great Books Foundation
A nonprofit educational organization

Copyright © 2012 by The Great Books Foundation

Chicago, Illinois

All rights reserved

ISBN 978-1-933147-96-3

9   8   7   6   5   4   3   2   1

Printed in the United States of America

Published and distributed by

THE GREAT BOOKS FOUNDATION

A nonprofit educational organization

35 East Wacker Drive, Suite 400

Chicago, IL 60601

www.greatbooks.org

Contents

THE FROGS GOT HOME LAST WEEK.

BEE! I'M EXPECTING YOU!

Emily Dickinson

Bee! I'm expecting you!
Was saying Yesterday
To Somebody you know
That you were due—

The Frogs got Home last Week—
Are settled, and at work—
Birds, mostly back—
The Clover warm and thick—

You'll get my Letter by
The seventeenth; Reply
Or better, be with me—
Yours, Fly.

THE FOX INVITED THE STORK TO DINNER.

THE FOX AND THE STORK

Aesop

At one time the Fox and the Stork were on visiting terms and seemed very good friends. So the Fox invited the Stork to dinner, and for a joke put nothing before her but some soup in a very shallow dish. This the Fox could easily lap up, but the Stork could only wet the end of her long bill in it, and left the meal as hungry as when she began. "I am sorry," said the Fox, "the soup is not to your liking."

"Pray do not apologize," said the Stork. "I hope you will return this visit, and come and dine with me soon." So a day was appointed when the Fox should visit the Stork; but when they were seated at table all that was for their dinner was contained in a very long-necked jar with a narrow mouth, in which the Fox could not insert his snout, so all he could manage to do was to lick the outside of the jar.

"I will not apologize for the dinner," said the Stork. "One bad turn deserves another."

I SEND THEM EAST AND WEST.

I Keep Six Honest Serving-Men

Rudyard Kipling

I keep six honest serving-men
  (They taught me all I knew);
Their names are What and Why and When
  And How and Where and Who.
I send them over land and sea,
  I send them east and west;
But after they have worked for me,
  I give them all a rest.

I let them rest from nine till five,
  For I am busy then,
As well as breakfast, lunch, and tea,
  For they are hungry men:
But different folk have different views,
  I know a person small—
She keeps ten million serving-men,
  Who get no rest at all!
She sends 'em abroad on her own affairs,
  From the second she opens her eyes—
One million Hows, two million Wheres,
  And seven million Whys!

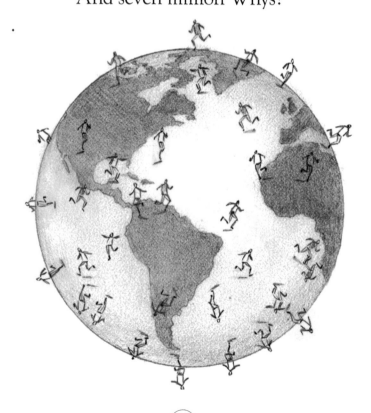

HE HADN'T GONE FAR WHEN HE SAW A TIGER.

THE BOY WHO GROWLED AT TIGERS

Donald Bisset

Once upon a time there was a little Indian boy whose name was Sudi, who growled at tigers.

"You be careful," his mother told him. "Tigers don't like being growled at."

But Sudi didn't care and, one day, when his mother was out shopping, he went for a walk to find a tiger to growl at.

He hadn't gone very far when he saw a tiger hiding behind a tree waiting for him to come along so that the tiger could chase him.

As soon as Sudi came up the tiger sprang out and growled, "GRRRRRGRRRRRRRGRRRRRGRRRRRRR."

And Sudi growled right back, "GRRRRGRRRRRRGRRRRRGRRRRRRRRR."

The tiger *was* annoyed!

"What does he think I am?" he thought. "A squirrel? A rabbit? A ocelot? Er . . . An ocelot?"

So, next day, when he saw Sudi coming, he sprang out from behind the tree and growled louder than ever "GRRRRGRRRRRGRRRRRGRR-RRRGRRRRR ! ! ! ! ! !"

"Nice tiger!" said Sudi, and stroked him.

The tiger couldn't bear it and went away and sharpened his claws and lashed his tail and practiced growling.

"I am a tiger!" he said. "T-I-G-E-R; TIGER, GRRR!" When he had finished he looked at his reflection in the water. There was a lovely yellow tiger with black stripes and a long tail. He growled again so loudly that he frightened even himself, and ran away. At last he stopped.

"What am I running away for?" he thought. "It's only me. Oh dear, that boy has upset me! I wonder why he growls at tigers?"

Next day, when Sudi passed, he stopped him.

"Why do you growl at tigers?" he said.

"Well," said Sudi, "it's because I'm shy really. And if I growl at tigers it sort of makes up for it, if you see what I mean."

"I see!" said the tiger.

"After all," said Sudi, "tigers are the fiercest animals in the world and it's very brave to growl at them."

The tiger *was* pleased.

"Fiercer than lions?" he said.

"Oh yes!" said Sudi.

"And bears?"

"Much fiercer."

The tiger purred and felt very friendly.

"You *are* a nice boy!" he said and gave him a lick.

After that they often went for walks together and growled at each other.

How We Worked Together in Discussion

Story or Poem: _____ Date: _____

Below are some things that a group should do when they have a discussion. For each one, fill in the circle that describes what your group did. Then talk about your answers together.

	A lot	A little	Not really
We shared interesting ideas.	○	○	○
We gave reasons for our ideas.	○	○	○
We listened to each other.	○	○	○
We made sure quiet people had a chance to share their ideas.	○	○	○
We learned a lot about the story.	○	○	○

Our goal for next time:

_____

_____

_____

_____

Acknowledgments

All possible care has been taken to trace ownership and secure permission for each selection in this series. The Great Books Foundation wishes to thank the following authors, publishers, and representatives for permission to reprint copyrighted material:

Bee! I'm expecting you!, from THE POEMS OF EMILY DICKINSON, by Emily Dickinson. Copyright © 1951, 1955, 1979, 1983 by the Presidents and Fellows of Harvard College. Reprinted by permission of the publishers and the Trustees of Amherst College.

The Boy Who Growled at Tigers, from ANOTHER TIME STORIES, by Donald Bisset. Copyright © 1970 by Donald Bisset. Reprinted by permission of A.M. Heath & Co Ltd.

Art Credits

Cover and interior art by Rich Lo. Copyright 2012 by Rich Lo.